2-D Airplane Shapes

Suzanne Barchers

CAPSTONE PRESS
a capstone imprint

First hardcover edition published in 2011 by
Capstone Press, a Capstone imprint
1710 Roe Crest Drive, North Mankato, MN 56003
www.capstonepub.com

Published in cooperation with Teacher Created Materials. Teacher Created Materials
is a copyright owner of the content contained in this title.

 This book was manufactured with paper containing
at least 10 percent post-consumer waste.

Editorial Credits

Dona Herweck Rice, editor-in-chief; Lee Aucoin, creative director; Sara Johnson,
senior editor; Jamey Acosta, associate editor; Neri Garcia and Gene Bentdahl,
designers; Stephanie Reid, photo editor; Rachelle Cracchiolo, M.A. Ed., publisher;
Eric Manske, production specialist

Library of Congress Cataloging-in-Publication Data
Barchers, Suzanne I.
  2-D airplane shapes / by Suzanne Barchers.
      p. cm.—(Real world math)
  Includes index.
  ISBN 978-1-4296-6844-6 (library binding)
  1. Geometry, Plane—Juvenile literature. 2. Shapes—Juvenile literature.
3. Airplanes—Juvenile literature. I. Title. II. Series.
  QA482.B36 2011
  516.22—dc22   2011001571

Image Credits

Alamy/First Light, 18
Dreamstime/Andres Rodriguez, 10 (all); Helen Filatova, 19; Ron Chapple
      Studios, 16; Soon Wee Meng, 8
Flickr/akoray, 11; chooyutshing, 7; gorgeoux, 9 (left); mrhayata, 15
Getty Images/AFP, 14; Jerry Driendl, 21
Shutterstock/Ambient Ideas, 13; Andresr, 20 (back); Carlos E. Santa Maria, 24;
      CROM, cover, 1; Eugene F, 17; Evan Meyer, 12 (all); Henrik Äijä, 26 (top);
      Herbert Kratky, 25; Light & Magic Photography, 23; Losevsky Pavel, 27;
      Margo Harrison, 22; Paul Prescott, 6; Randy Mayes, 20 (front); Rob Wilson, 26
      (bottom); ssguy, 5; Stian Iversen, 9 (right)
Tim Bradley, 28

Printed in the United States of America in Stevens Point, Wisconsin.
072012   006856R

Table of Contents

Two-Dimensional Shapes

There are many different kinds of shapes. Some shapes are **two-dimensional**. That means that the shapes are flat. Some have sides and **vertices**. A vertex is the point where sides meet.

> The shapes below are 2-D, two-dimensional.

Two-dimensional shapes can be found when you travel. Are you going to an airport? You can do more than wait for your plane while you are there. Take a close look at all the shapes you can find.

Finding Circles

Look up! You will not want to miss the **circles** at the Madrid airport. The ceiling is full of them. Rows of lights in these circles seem to lead you on your way.

This huge circle greets you at an airport in Singapore.

Architects are people who **design** buildings. They use lines and shapes in their plans. They often use circles, rectangles, triangles, and squares.

The control tower at the Singapore airport has a golden ball on top.

If you know you will have a long wait, bring your suit. You can take a swim in the pool on the roof of the Singapore airport. Then relax in the hot tub. It is one big circle.

LET'S EXPLORE MATH

A circle is flat and perfectly round. The distance from the center of the circle to the edge is always the same. Look at these shapes. Which ones are circles?

1.   2.   3.   4.

Finding Triangles

Take a drive to this airport in London. You will see a lot of **triangles**. Their shape gives strength to the building's structure.

Inside you see even more triangles. They are a good design choice. They give you something to look at.

A triangle has 3 sides and 3 vertices. The sides can be the same length. Or the sides can be different lengths.

vertex

side

What is the first shape you see at the Denver airport? Triangles! Does it make you think of the tall mountains nearby? The designers hope so!

The roof of the airport is made of strong cloth shaped into triangles.

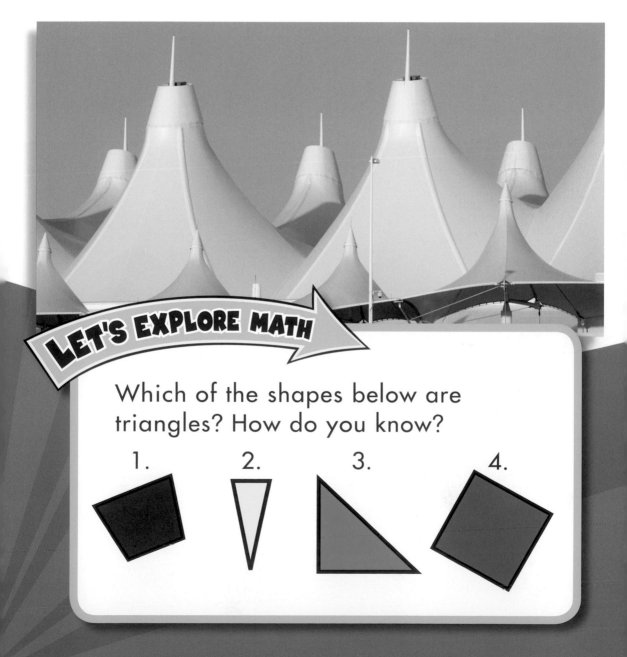

LET'S EXPLORE MATH

Which of the shapes below are triangles? How do you know?

1.   2.   3.   4.

Finding Rectangles

Have you ever seen a man-made island? This airport was built on one. It is in Japan. The first part looks like one big **rectangle**.

A rectangle has 4 sides. The newer part of the airport has 6 sides. It has a long runway!

A shape with 6 sides is called a **hexagon**. The shapes below are hexagons.

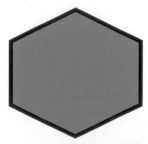

A lot of shapes have 4 sides. A rectangle must have **parallel** sides too. A runway has parallel lines. Look at the sides of the one below. They do not meet. They just stop at some point.

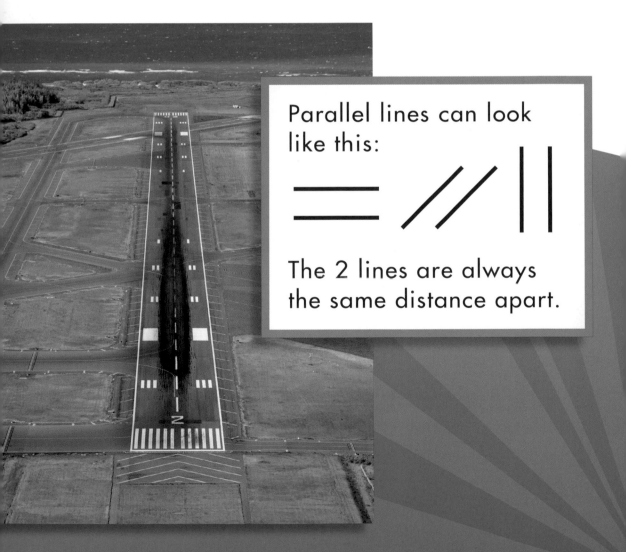

Parallel lines can look like this:

The 2 lines are always the same distance apart.

Long parallel lines look like they meet. But they will never meet.

a. Which shapes below have parallel lines?

b. Which shapes are rectangles? How do you know?

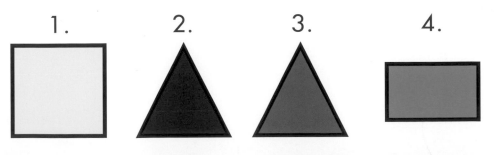

1. 2. 3. 4.

Finding Squares

Look up. Look down. Look out the windows. You cannot miss the **squares** at this airport in Canada.

Squares are often used for floors and ceilings. The sides of squares are all equal. That makes it easy to place them together on the floor.

length

width

The roof at an airport in Paris is made of squares too. But these squares are different. They are made of strong glass.

The design of this airport in Costa Rica is fun. It has circles inside the squares.

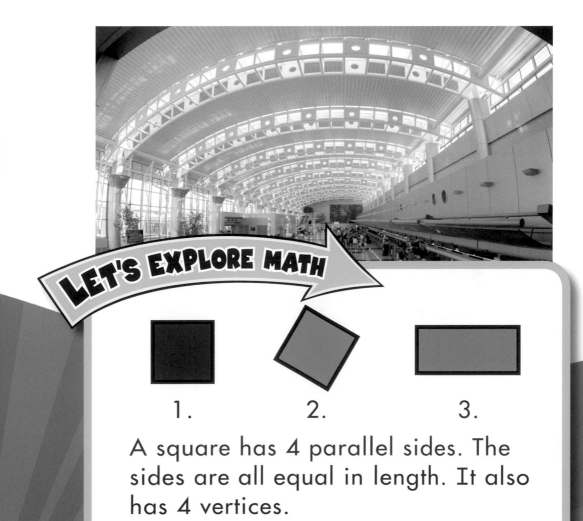

LET'S EXPLORE MATH

1.   2.   3.

A square has 4 parallel sides. The sides are all equal in length. It also has 4 vertices.

a. How many vertices and sides does each shape above have?

b. Which shapes above are squares? How do you know?

On the Plane

You have seen shapes in all kinds of airports. What shapes can you see in airplanes? The earliest planes had wings that looked like rectangles.

Now airplane wings look more like triangles. This jet has huge wings!

Peek inside the cockpit when you board your plane. You may see the square screens that the pilots use.

Your seating area also has shapes. You may sit on a rectangle. You may watch a movie on a rectangle. Look up. There are rectangles above you too.

Take time to look at all the signs.
Each sign has a shape.

The next time you take a trip, you will have plenty to do. You can probably find hundreds of shapes. You just need to look!

Train Shapes

Shapes are found in many places and on many things. This is a drawing of a train that was used in the 1800s. Can you find all the shapes in the drawing?

a. How many circles are in the drawing?

b. How many triangles are in the drawing?

c. How many squares are in the drawing?

d. How many rectangles are in the drawing?

e. How many shapes are there in total?

Solve It!

Use the steps below to help you solve the problems.

Step 1: Start at the left. Count all the circles from left to right. Write how many circles you counted.

Step 2: Repeat Step 1 and count all the triangles. Write how many triangles you counted.

Step 3: Start on the left again. This time look for squares. Write how many squares you counted.

Step 4: Start on the left again. Look for rectangles first in the locomotive. Be careful! Some are very small. Then count the rectangles in the freight car. Write how many rectangles you counted.

Step 5: To find the total, add up all the shapes you counted.

Glossary

circles—flat, round shapes

design—a plan for something or to create that plan

hexagon—a flat shape with 6 sides and 6 vertices

parallel—lines that are the same distance apart and never overlap

rectangle—a flat shape with 4 vertices and 2 sets of equal parallel sides

squares—flat shapes with 4 vertices and 4 equal sides

triangles—flat shapes with 3 sides and 3 vertices

two-dimensional—a flat shape that has both length and width

vertices—the points where 2 or more sides meet

 Index

Let's Explore Math

Page 9:
Shapes 2 and 4 are circles.

Page 13:
Shapes 2 and 3 are triangles; answers will vary, but should include that triangles have 3 sides and 3 vertices.

Page 17:
a. Shapes 1 and 4 have parallel lines.

b. Shapes 1 and 4 are rectangles; answers will vary, but should include that rectangles have 4 sides and 4 vertices.

Page 21:
a. 4 vertices and 4 sides

b. Shapes 1 and 2 are squares; answers will vary, but should include that squares have 4 vertices and 4 equal sides.

Pages 28–29:

Problem-Solving Activity

Answers will vary for all problems.